STRUM & SING

Carole King

Cover photo by Michael Ochs Archives/Getty Images

ISBN 978-1-4803-1450-4

HAL•LEONARD®
CORPORATION

7777 W. BLUEMOUND RD. P.O. BOX 13819 MILWAUKEE, WI 53213

In Australia Contact:
Hal Leonard Australia Pty. Ltd.
4 Lentara Court
Cheltenham, Victoria, 3192 Australia
Email: ausadmin@halleonard.com.au

Visit Hal Leonard Online at
www.halleonard.com

Contents

Beautiful

Words and Music by
Carole King

(Capo 3rd fret)

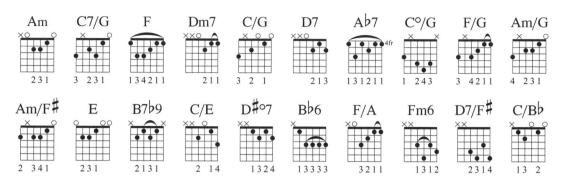

Chorus 1

| Am | | C7/G | F | Dm7 |

You got to get up ev - 'ry morn - ing with a smile on your face

| C/G | Am | D7 | |

And show the world   all the love in your heart.

| F | | C/G | |

Then people gonna treat you bet - ter. You're gonna find, yes, you will,

| Ab7 | | |

That you're beau - tiful   as you feel.

| C/G | C°/G | F/G | | ||

Verse 1

| Am | Am/G | Am/F# | F |

Waiting at the station with a work - day wind a-blow - ing,

| E | B7b9 | E | | |

I've got   nothing to do   but watch the passers-by.

| Dm7 | | C/E | |

Mirrored in their faces I see   frustration growing,

| D#°7 | | E | | ||

And they   don't see it showing. Why do I?

Repeat Chorus 1

Interlude   C |B♭6 |F/A |F   C/E |

                      Dm7 |C/E |Ab7 | ||

Verse 2

Am |Am/G |Am/F♯ |F
I have often asked   myself the rea - son for the sad - ness

        |E |B7♭9 |E | |
In a world   where tears are just a lull - aby.

Dm7 | |C/E |
If there's any an - swer, maybe love   can end the mad - ness;

    |D♯°7 | |E | ||
Maybe not, oh, but we   can only try.

Chorus 2

Am |C7/G |F |Dm7
   You got to get up ev'ry morn - ing with a smile on your face

    |C/G |Am |D7   C/E |Fm6   D7/F♯
And show the world all   the love in your heart.

    |F | |C/G |
Then people gonna treat you bet - ter. You're gonna find, yes, you will,

    |Ab7 | |Dm7 |
That you're beau - tiful,   you're beau - tiful,

    |D♯°7 | |C/G | |F/G | ||
You're beau - tiful   as you feel.

Outro   C |C/B♭ |

F |Dm7 |C/G |Am |

D7   C/E |Fm6 D7/F♯ |F | |

C/G | |Ab7 | |

Begin fade   *Fade out*

Dm7 | |D♯°7 | |C/G ||

Crying in the Rain

Words and Music by
Carole King and Howard Greenfield

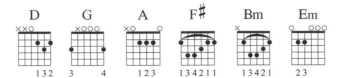

Intro   D

Verse 1

D   G |A   D |
I'll never let you see

D   G |A   D |
The way my broken heart is hurting me.

D   G |F#   Bm |G |
I've got my pride and I know how to hide   all my sorrow and pain;

A N.C. |Bm   A Bm| ||
I'll do my crying in the rain.

Verse 2

D   G |A   D |
If I wait for cloudy skies,

D   G |A   D |
You won't know the rain from the tears in my eyes.

D   G |F#   Bm |G |
You'll never know that I still love you so.   Though the heartaches remain,

A N.C. |Bm   A Bm| ||
I'll do my crying in the rain.

Bridge

G |Em
Raindrops falling from heaven
  |A |D
Could never wash away my miser - y.
  |Bm |G
But since we're not together I look for stormy weather
  |A | ‖
To hide these tears I hope you'll never see.

Verse 3

D   G |A   D |
  Some - day when my crying's done,
D   G |A   D
I'm gonna wear a smile and walk in the sun.
|D   G |F♯   Bm |G |
I may be a fool, but till then, darling, you'll never see me complain.
A |Bm   A Bm |
  I'll do my crying in the rain.
N.C. |Bm   A Bm |
    I'll do my crying in the rain.
N.C. | Bm |D   ‖
    I'll do my crying in the rain.

Go Away, Little Girl

Words and Music by
Gerry Goffin and Carole King

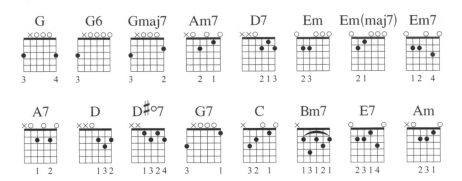

Intro

|G |G6 |Gmaj7 |G6

Verse 1

‖G |G6 |Gmaj7 |G6
Go a-way, little girl.   Go a-way, little girl.
|Am7   D7 |Am7 D7 |G |
I'm not sup-posed to be a-lone with you.
|Em |Em(maj7) |Em7 |A7
I know that your lips are sweet,   but our lips must never meet.
|D   D#°7 |Em7   A7 |D7 |
I be-long to someone else and I must be true.

Verse 2

‖G |G6 |Gmaj7 |G6
Oh, go a-way, little girl.   Go a-way, little girl.
|Am7   D7 |Am7 D7 |G Gmaj7 |G7
It's hurting me more each minute that you de-lay.
|C |Am7 |Bm7 |E7
When you are near me like this,   you're much too hard to resist.
|Am7 |D7 |G |D7   ‖
So go a-way, little girl, be-fore I beg you to stay.

Bridge

G |G6 |Gmaj7 |G6 |

Go a - way.   Please don't stay.

Am7   D7 |Am7   D7 |G   Gmaj7 |G7

It'll never work out.

Verse 3

               ||C |Am7 |Bm7 |E7

When you are near me like this,   you're much too hard to resist.

       |C |Am7 |Bm7 |E7

So go a - way, little girl.   Call it a day, little girl.

           |Am7 |D7 |G |

Oh, please, go a - way, little girl, be - fore I beg you to stay.

   |G | ||

Go a - way.

Hey, Girl

Words and Music by
Carole King and Gerry Goffin

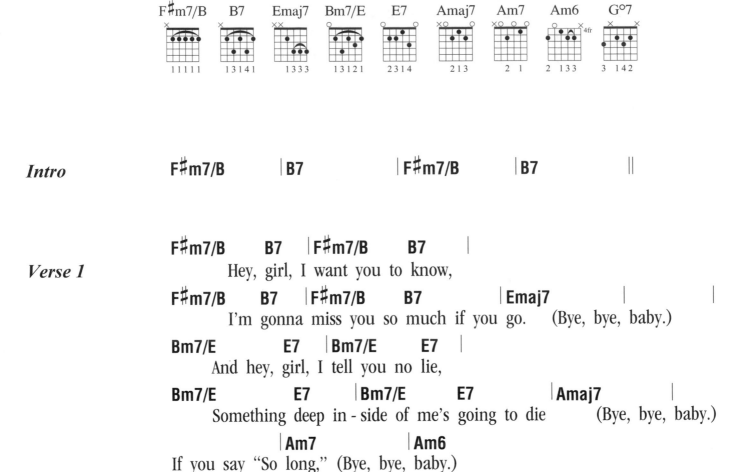

Intro   F♯m7/B |B7 |F♯m7/B |B7   ‖

Verse 1

F♯m7/B   B7 |F♯m7/B   B7 |
     Hey, girl, I want you to know,

F♯m7/B   B7 |F♯m7/B   B7 |Emaj7 | |
     I'm gonna miss you so much if you go.   (Bye, bye, baby.)

Bm7/E   E7 |Bm7/E   E7 |
     And hey, girl, I tell you no lie,

Bm7/E   E7 |Bm7/E   E7 |Amaj7 |
     Something deep in - side of me's going to die   (Bye, bye, baby.)

    |Am7 |Am6
If you say "So long," (Bye, bye, baby.)

    |Emaj7 | |G°7 | ‖
If this is "Goodbye."   (Bye, bye, baby.) Oh,   oh.

Verse 2

F♯m7/B   B7 | F♯m7/B   B7 |
Hey, girl, this can't be true.

F♯m7/B   B7 | F♯m7/B   B7 |Emaj7 | |
How am I sup - posed to ex - ist without   you? (Bye, bye, baby.)

Bm7/E   E7 |Bm7/E   E7 |
Hey, girl, now don't put me on.

Bm7/E   E7 |Bm7/E   E7 |Amaj7 |
What's gonna happen to me when you're   gone? (Bye, bye, baby.)

    |Am7 |Am6
How will I live? (Bye, bye, baby.)

     |Emaj7 |
How can I go on? (Bye, bye, baby.)

    |G°7 | ‖
How can I go on? (Bye, bye, baby.) Oh.

Interlude

F♯m7/B B7 | F♯m7/B B7 | F♯m7/B B7 | F♯m7/B B7 | Emaj7 | ‖
(Bye, bye, baby.)

Verse 3

Bm7/E   E7 |Bm7/E   E7 |
Hey, girl, now sit yourself down.

Bm7/E   E7 |Bm7/E   E7 |Amaj7 |
I'm not a - shamed to get down on the ground, (Bye, bye, baby.)

 |Am7 |Am6
And then (Bye, bye, baby.)

    |Emaj7 |
Beg you to stay. (Bye, bye, baby.)

Outro

    ‖: F♯m7/B |
Don't go a - way. (Bye, bye, baby.)   *Repeat and fade*

  |Emaj7 | :‖
Hey, girl. (Bye, bye, baby.) No, I beg ya, please, don't go a -

Home Again

Words and Music by
Carole King

Intro

| A | G/A | | A | G/A | |

Verse 1

A   E/A   D/A   A
Sometimes I wonder if I'm ever gonna make it home   again;

D   A/C♯   Bm7 |A   D/A |
It's so far   and out   of sight.

A   E/A   D/A   A
I really need someone to talk to, and nobody else

D   A/C♯   Bm7 |A
Knows how to com - fort me tonight.

Chorus 1

F♯m |A7
Snow is cold, rain   is wet;

D   A/C♯ |B7sus4 B7   D/E E7 |
Chills my soul right to the mar - row.

A   E/A   D/A A
I won't be happy till I see you alone   again,

D   A/C♯   Bm7   D/E |A   G/A   D/A
Till I'm home   again   and feel - ing right.

A   G/A   D/A

Interlude

```
A          E/A            |            D/A    A    |

D          G    D    |A         D/A              |

A          E/A            |            D/A    A    |

D          G    D    |A                          ||
```

Chorus 2

```
F#m                |A7              |
Snow is cold, rain     is wet;
D        A/C#              |B7sus4 B7    D/E  E7   |
Chills my soul right to the mar  -  row.
A          E/A              |        D/A    A  |
   I won't be happy till I see  you alone    again,
D          A/C#    Bm7      D/E  |A          |
Till I'm home    again    and feel - ing right,
D      A/C#        Bm7      D/E  |A
Till I'm home again     and feel - ing right.
      |D      A/C#    Bm7      D/E  |A      G/A      D/A   |
I wanna be home      again     and feel - ing right.
A      G/A      D/A  |A      G/A      D/A    A  |       ||
```

I Feel the Earth Move

Words and Music by
Carole King

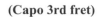

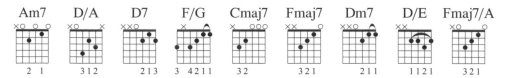

Intro   **Am7** | **D/A** |**Am7** | **D/A**

Chorus 1

‖**Am7** | **D/A**
I feel the earth move under my feet;
          |**Am7** |
I feel the sky tumbling down.
               |**D7** |
I feel my heart start to trembling
          |**Am7** |**D/A**
Whenever you're around.

Verse 1

F/G Cmaj7 | **Fmaj7** | |
Ooh, ba - by, when I see   your face,
Dm7 |**F/G**
Mellow as the month of May,
     |**Cmaj7**   **Fmaj7** |
Oh, dar - ling, I can't stand   it
               |**Dm7** |**F/G   D/E**
When you look at me that way.

Repeat Chorus 1

          Am7 | **N.C.**   ‖

Interlude **Am7** |**D7** |**Am7** |**D7** |

Am7 |**D7** |**Am7** |**D7**

F/G Cmaj7 ‖ **Fmaj7** |
Verse 2 Ooh, dar - ling, when you're near me
          |**Dm7** |**F/G**
And you ten - derly call my name,
    |**Cmaj7** **Fmaj7** |
I know that my e - mo - tions
    |**Dm7** |**F/G**
Are some - thing I just can't tame.
       D/E |**Am7** |
I've just got to have you, baby.
    D/A |**Am7** | **D/A**
Ah, ah, ah. Ah, ah, ah, yeah.

      ‖**Am7** | **D/A**
Chorus 2 I feel the earth move under my feet;
      |**Am7** | **D/A**
I feel the sky tumbling down, a - tumbling down.
    |**Am7** | **D/A**
I feel the earth move under my feet;
    |**Am7** | **D/A**
I feel the sky tumbling down, a - tumbling down.
    |**Am7** |**D7**
I just lose control
      |**Am7** |**D7**
Down to my very soul.
      |**Am7** |**D7**
I get-a hot and cold
     |**Am7** | **D/A**
All o - ver, all over, all o - ver, all over.

Chorus 3

|| **Am7** | **D/A**
I feel the earth move under my feet;

| **Am7** | **D/A**
I feel the sky tumbling down, a - tumbling down.

| **Am7** | **D/A**
I feel the earth move under my feet;

| **Am7** | **D/A**
I feel the sky tumbling down, a - tumbling down,

| **Am7** | **D/A** |
A-tumb - ling down, a-tumbling down,   a-tumbling down,

Fmaj7/A | **D/A** ||
Tumbling down.

It's Too Late

Words and Music by
Carole King and Toni Stern

(Capo 5th fret)

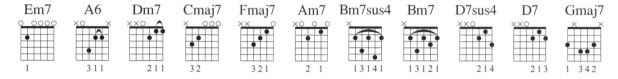

Em7   A6   Dm7   Cmaj7   Fmaj7   Am7   Bm7sus4   Bm7   D7sus4   D7   Gmaj7

Intro |**Em7**   **A6** | |**Em7**   **A6** | ||

Verse 1

Em7 |**A6** |
Stayed in bed all morning just to pass the time.

Em7 |**A6** |
   There's something wrong here, there can be no denying.

Em7 |**Dm7** |**Cmaj7** |
One of us is changing or maybe we just stopped try - ing.

Chorus 1

        ||**Fmaj7** |**Cmaj7**
And it's too   late, baby, now it's too late,

        |**Fmaj7** |**Cmaj7** |
Though we really did try to make   it.

Fmaj7 |**Cmaj7** |
Something inside has died   and I can't hide

Am7 |**Bm7sus4** |
  And I just can't fake   it.

Bm7 |**Em7**   **A6** | |**Em7**   **A6** |
Oh,   no,   no, no, no. (No, no, no, no.)

Verse 2

||Em7 |A6

It used to be so easy living here with you.

Em7 |A6

You were light and breezy and I knew   just what to do.

|Em7 |Dm7 |Cmaj7

Now you look so unhappy and I   feel like a fool.

Chorus 2

||Fmaj7 |Cmaj7

And it's too   late, baby, now it's too late,

|Fmaj7 |Cmaj7

Though we really did try to make   it.

Fmaj7 |Cmaj7

Something inside has died   and I can't hide

Am7 |D7sus4

  And I just can't fake   it.

Interlude 1

    D7 ||Gmaj7 |Cmaj7 |Fmaj7 |Em7 |

Oh,   no,   no.

Dm7 |Cmaj7 |Am7 |Bm7sus4 Bm7 |

Em7   A6 | |Em7   A6 | |

Em7   A6 | |Em7   A6 | ||

Verse 3

Em7 |A6
There'll be good times again for me and you,

    |Em7 |A6
But we just can't stay together; don't you feel it, too?

      |Em7 |Dm7 |Cmaj7 |
Still, I'm glad for what we had   and how I once loved   you.

Repeat Chorus 2

Interlude 2

    D7   ‖Gmaj7 |Cmaj7 |Fmaj7 |Em7 |
Oh,   no,   no, no, no,   no.
Dm7 |Cmaj7 |Am7 |D7sus4

Outro

    D7   ‖Gmaj7 |Cmaj7 |Gmaj7 |Cmaj7
It's too late,   ba - by, it's too late,   now, dar - ling,

      |Gmaj7 | ‖
It's too late.

I'm into Something Good

Words and Music by
Gerry Goffin and Carole King

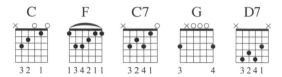

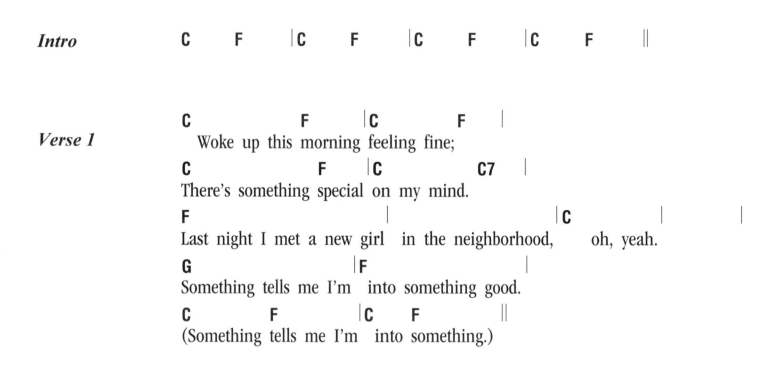

Intro

C F |C F |C F |C F ||

Verse 1

C   F |C   F |
    Woke up this morning feeling fine;

C   F |C   C7 |
There's something special on my mind.

F | |C | |
Last night I met a new girl   in the neighborhood,   oh, yeah.

G |F |
Something tells me I'm   into something good.

C   F |C   F ||
(Something tells me I'm   into something.)

Verse 2

```
  C                    F       |C          F       |
She's the kind of girl who's not too shy,
  C        F      |C              C7     |
And I can tell I'm her kind of guy.
  F                      |                    |
She danced close to me   like I hoped she would.
  C                         |               |
   (She danced with me like I hoped she would.)
  G                     |F              |
Something tells me I'm   into something good.
  C        F        |C    F          ||
(Something tells me I'm   into something.)
```

Bridge

```
  G                      |
   We only danced for a minute or two,
                |C          F    |C              |
And then she stuck close to me the whole night through.
  G          |            |
   Can I be falling in love?
D7                      |F          |
(She's everything I've been dreaming of.)
G                          |D7        G    ||
   She's every - thing I've been dreaming of.
```

Verse 3

```
            C              F         |C              F
I walked her home and she held my hand.
  |C            F        |C              C7
I knew it couldn't be just a one-night stand.
    |F                        |                        |
So I asked to see her next week   and she told me I could.
  C                                  |                        |
   (I asked to see her and she told me I could.)
  G                    |F                   |
Something tells me I'm   into something good.
  C        F          |C    F            |
(Something tells me I'm   into something.
  C        F          |C    F            ||
Something tells me I'm   into something.)
```

Interlude

```
  G           |           |           |         |C    F   |C           |
Ah.
  G           |               |D7        |F    G    ||
```

Verse 4

```
  C              F         |C              F
I walked her home and she held my hand.
  |C            F        |C              C7
I knew it couldn't be just a one-night stand.
    |F                        |                        |
So I asked to see her next week   and she told me I could.
  C                                  |                ||
   (I asked to see her and she told me I could.)
```

Outro

```
G                        |F                   |
Something tells me I'm  into something good.
C        F         |C    F          |
(Something tells me I'm  into something.)
G                        |F                   |
Something tells me I'm  into something good.
C        F         |C
(Something tells me I'm  in -)
   F       |G      |F                |
To something good, oh, yeah, something good.
C        F         |C
(Something tells me I'm  in -)
   F       |G         |F            |C       ||
To something good, something good, something good.
```

The Loco-Motion

Words and Music by
Gerry Goffin and Carole King

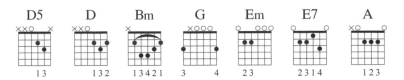

Intro | D5 | | | ‖

Verse 1

D |Bm |
Everybody's doing my brand-new dance now.

D |Bm
   (Come on baby, do   the loco-motion.)

|D |Bm |
I know you'll get to like it if you give it a chance now.

D |Bm
   (Come on baby, do   the loco-motion.)

 |G |Em
My little baby sister can do it with ease;

 |G |E7
It's easier than learning your A-B-C's.

 |D |A   ‖
So come on, come on, do   the loco-motion with me.

Bridge

```
       D          |                    |G
         You gotta swing your hips now.
              |G
Come on, baby,
              |D          |
Jump up,    jump back.
              |A                    |              ||
Oh, well, I think you've got the knack.    Wow, wow.
```

Verse 2

```
D                        |Bm                    |
Now that you can do it, let's make a chain now.
D                   |Bm
   (Come on baby, do    the loco-motion.)
  |D                        |Bm              |
A chug-a chug-a motion like a railroad train now.
D                   |Bm          |
   (Come on baby, do    the loco-motion.)
G                        |Em
Do it nice and easy now, don't lose control,
  |G                      |E7          |
A little bit of rhythm and a lot of soul.
D              |A                    ||
Come on baby, do   the loco-motion with me.
```

Interlude

```
D              |              |G          |              |

D              |              |A          |              ||
                                          Yay, yay, yay, yeah.
```

Verse 3

```
D                         |Bm           |
Move around the floor in a loco-motion.
D               |Bm                |
  (Come on baby, do    the loco-motion.)
D                      |Bm               |
Do it holding hands if you get the notion.
D                    |Bm              |
  (Come on baby, do    the loco-motion.)
        |G                        |Em
There's never been a dance that's so easy to do.
    |G                        |E7
It even makes you happy when you're feeling blue.
    |D                    |A                        ||
So come on, come on, do   the loco-motion with me.
```

Outro

```
D                        |                    |
  (Come on.) You gotta swing your hips now.
G                            |
  (Come on,) That's right. (do   the loco-motion.)
            |D               |
You're doing fine!  (Come on, do   the loco-motion.)
        |G                   |
Come on, baby. (Come on, do   the loco-motion.)
        |D                        |
Jump up,  (Come on,) jump back. (do   the loco-motion.)
            |G              |            |D        ||
You're looking good. (Come on, do   the loco-motion.)
```

Pleasant Valley Sunday

Words and Music by
Gerry Goffin and Carole King

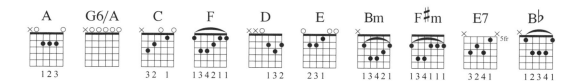

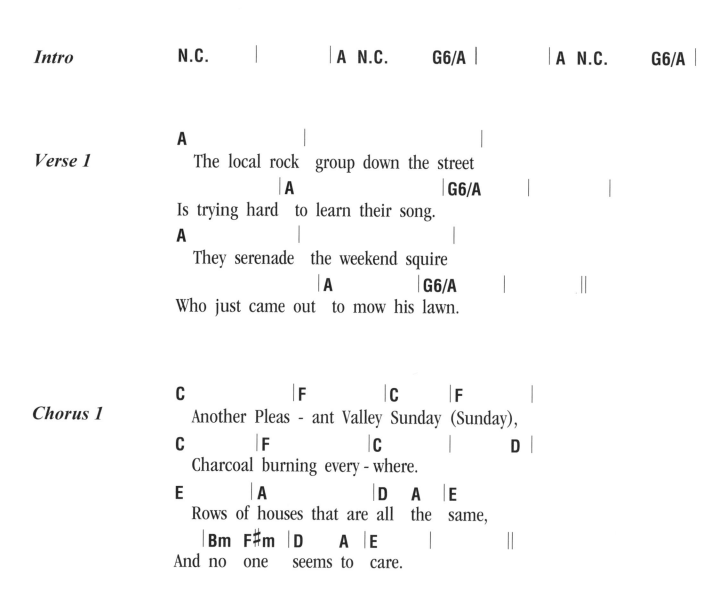

Intro

N.C. | |A N.C. G6/A | |A N.C. G6/A | ‖

Verse 1

A | |
  The local rock group down the street
  |A |G6/A | |
Is trying hard to learn their song.
A | |
  They serenade the weekend squire
  |A |G6/A | ‖
Who just came out to mow his lawn.

Chorus 1

C |F |C |F |
Another Pleas - ant Valley Sunday (Sunday),
C |F |C | D|
Charcoal burning every - where.
E |A |D A |E
Rows of houses that are all the same,
|Bm F#m |D A |E | ‖
And no one seems to care.

Verse 2

A | |
See Missus Gray;   she's proud today
              |A |G6/A | |
Because her ros - es are in bloom.
A | |
And Mister Green, he's so serene;
            |A |G6/A | ||
He's got a T - V in every room.

Chorus 2

C |F |C |F |
Another Pleas - ant Valley Sunday (Sunday)
C |F |C | D|
Here in status symbol land.
E |A |D A |E
Mothers com - plain about how hard life is
   |Bm F#m |D A |E | ||
And the kids just   don't under - stand.

Bridge

E7 | |
Creature comfort goals,
E7 | |
They only numb my soul
E7 | | | |
And make it hard for me to see. (La la la.)
E7 | |
My thoughts all seem to stray
E7 | |
To places far away.
E7 | |E7 | |
I need a change of scener - y.
A   G6/A | |A   G6/A | ||

Interlude

A | |
Ta ta ta ta, ta ta ta ta,

|A |G6/A | |
Ta ta ta ta, ta ta ta ta. (Ah.)

A | |
Ta ta ta ta, ta ta ta ta,

|A |G6/A | ||
Ta ta ta ta, ta ta ta ta. (Ah.)

Chorus 3

C |F |C |F |
Another Pleas - ant Valley Sunday (Sunday),

C |F |C | |
Charcoal burning every - where.

F |B♭ |F |B♭ |
Another Pleas - ant Valley Sunday.

F |B♭ |F | |
Here in status symbol land.

A G6/A | |A G6/A | ||

Repeat and fade

‖:A |G6/A |A |G6/A :‖

Outro
Another Pleas - ant Valley Sunday.

Now and Forever
(from the Columbia Motion Picture A LEAGUE OF THEIR OWN)

Words and Music by
Carole King

(Capo 1st fret)

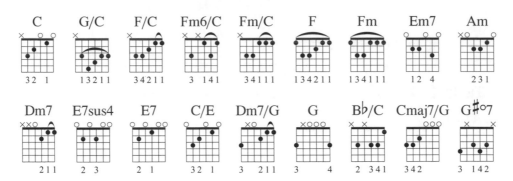

Intro

C |G/C |F/C |Fm6/C

Verse 1

          ||C |G/C
Now and for - ever, you are a part of me,

       |F/C   Fm/C |C
And the mem'ry cuts like a knife.

            |C |G/C
Didn't we find the ecstasy, didn't we share the daylight

        |F   Fm |C
When you walked in - to my life.

        |Em7 |Am
Now and for - ever, I'll re - member

   |Dm7   E7sus4   E7 |Am |
All the promises still   un - bro - ken,

F |C/E |
    And think about all the words be - tween us

Dm7 |Dm7/G   G
    That never needed to be spo - ken.

Verse 2

    ‖C |G/C
We had a mo - ment, just one   moment,

    |B♭/C |Am
That will last beyond a dream, beyond a lifetime.

    |Em7 |
We are the lucky ones.

Dm7   E7sus4 E7 |Am Cmaj7/G |F   C/E
  Some people never get to do all   we got to do.

           |Dm7 |Dm7/G   G|C |G/C C   ‖
Now and for - ever,   I will always think of you.

Bridge

F |C/E |
Didn't we come together, didn't we live together,

Dm7 |C |
Didn't we cry together, didn't we play together,

Em7 |
Didn't we love together;

Am |Dm7 |Dm7/G
  And together we lit   up the world.

Verse 3

     ‖C |G/C
I miss the tears, I miss the laughter,

    |B♭/C |Am
I miss the day we met and all that followed after.

    |Em7 |Dm7
Sometimes I   wish I could always be with you

  E7sus4 E7 |Am Cmaj7/G |F   C/E
The way we used to do.   Oh,

         |Dm7 |Dm7/G   G♯°7 |Am |Cmaj7/G
Now and for - ever,   I will always think of   you.

       |F   C/E |Dm7 Dm7/G |C |G/C |F/C |Fm6/C |
Now and for - ever,   I will always be with you. Oh.

C |G/C |F/C |Fm6/C |C   ‖

One Fine Day

Words and Music by
Gerry Goffin and Carole King

G   Em   C   D7sus4   D   Cm   Dm7   Cmaj7   C6   Em7   A   D7

Intro

G |Em |C |D7sus4 |

G |Em |
(Shoo-be-do-be-do-be - do-be-do wah, wah.

C |D7sus4 ||
Shoo-be-do-be-do-be - do-be-do wah, wah.)

Verse 1

G | |D | |
One fine day   you'll look at me,

Em | |Cm | |
   And you will know our love was   meant to be.

G |Em |C |D |
One fine day   you're gonna want me

    |G |Em |C |D7sus4 ||
For your girl.

Verse 2

G | |D | |
The arms I long for   will open wide,

Em | |Cm | |
   And you'll be proud to have me   right by your side.

G |Em |C |D |
One fine day   you're gonna want me

    |G |C |G | ||
For your girl.

Bridge

Dm7 |G |Dm7 |G |
Though I know you're the kind of boy

C |Cmaj7 |C6 |Cmaj7 |
Who only wants to run a - round,

Em7 |A |Em7 |A |
I'll keep waiting, and someday, darling,

D7 | | |
You'll come to me when you want to settle down.

Verse 3

‖G | |D | |
Oh, one fine day we'll meet once more,

Em | |Cm | |
And then you'll want the love you threw away be - fore.

G |Em |C |D
One fine day you're gonna want me

|G |Em |C |D7sus4 ‖
For your girl.

Interlude

G | |D | |

Em | |Cm | |
One fine day you're gonna want me

G |Em |C |D
For your girl. (One fine day.)

|G |Em |C |D ‖
One fine

Outro

Repeat and fade

‖:G |Em |C |D :‖
Day. Oh, yeah. One fine

33

Really Rosy

Words and Music by
Carole King and Maurice Sendak

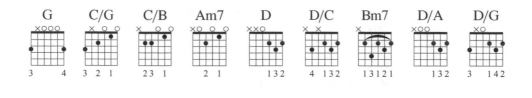

Intro

G |C/G |G |C/G ||

Chorus 1

G |C/G
I'm really Rosy,
  |G |C/G |
And I'm Rosy Real.
G |C/G
You better believe me,
   |G |C/G
I'm a great big deal.
   |G |C/G |G |C/G
Be - lieve   me. (Be - lieve   me.)

Verse 1

   ||C |C/B |
I'm a star from afar off the golden coast.
Am7 |C/G
Beat that drum, make that toast
 |**D** D/C |**Bm7** D/A
To Ro - sy the most.
   |G |C/G |G |C/G
Be - lieve   me. (Be - lieve   me.)

Verse 2

  ‖**G** |**D/G**

I can sing "Tea for Two" and "Two for Tea."

   |**C/G** |**G**

I can act "To be or not to be."

   |**C** **C/B** |**Am7**   **C/G**

I can tap a - cross the Tap - pan Zee.

   |**D**   **D/C** |**Bm7**   **D/A** |

Hey, can't you see? I'm ter - rific at ev - 'rything.

D **D/C** |**Bm7**   **D/A**

No star shines so bright as me.

Chorus 2

   ‖**G** |**C/G**

I'm Ro - sy.

   |**G** |**C/G** |**G** |**C/G** ‖

Be - lieve me. (Be - lieve me.)

Outro   **G** |**C/G** |**G** |**C/G** |

           G |**C/G** |**G**   ‖

Smackwater Jack

Words and Music by
Gerry Goffin and Carole King

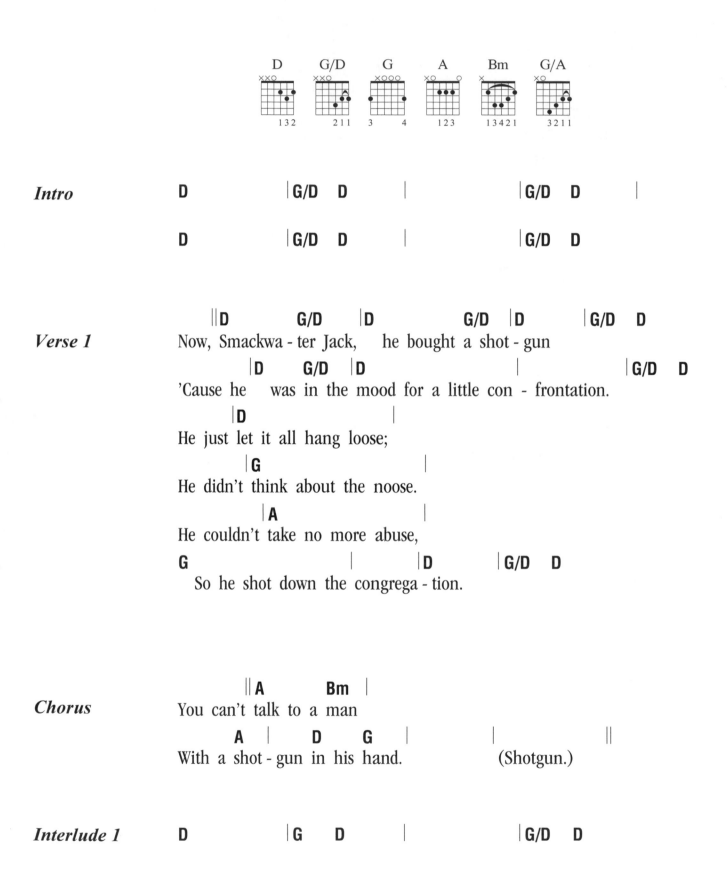

Intro

D |G/D   D | |G/D   D |

D |G/D   D | |G/D   D

Verse 1

‖D   G/D |D   G/D |D |G/D   D
Now, Smackwa - ter Jack,   he bought a shot - gun

       |D   G/D |D | |G/D   D
'Cause he   was in the mood for a little con - frontation.

       |D |
He just let it all hang loose;

       |G |
He didn't think about the noose.

       |A |
He couldn't take no more abuse,

G | |D |G/D   D
   So he shot down the congrega - tion.

Chorus

‖A   Bm |
You can't talk to a man

      A | D   G | | ‖
With a shot - gun in his hand.   (Shotgun.)

Interlude 1

D |G   D | |G/D   D

Verse 2

```
      ‖D        G/D     |D                    |        |G/D   D
      Now, Big Jim, the chief,  stood for law and ord - er.
               |D              G/D    |D                  |        |G/D   D
      He called    for the guard to come  and surround the bor - der.
              |D                    |
      Now from his bulldog mouth,
               |G                   |
      As he led  the posse south,
                  |A                      |G                |
      Came the cry, "We got to ride to clean   up the streets
      G                           |D        |G/D   D
         For our wives and our daugh - ters."
```

Chorus 2

```
             ‖A        Bm  |
      You can't talk to a man
                  A   |    D      G    |          |
      When he don't  want to under - stand,
      G              |D        |G   D       ‖
      No, no, no, no, no, no.
```

Interlude 2

```
      D              |G   D      |            |G/D   D      |
      D              |G   D    |G/A          |            |
      D              |G/D   D     |            |G/D   D
```

Verse 3

```
       ‖D        G/D   |D            G/D  |D        |G/D   D
```
The ac - count of the cap - ture wasn't in the pa - pers.
```
                |D               G/D   |D            |
```
But you know,   they hanged old   Smack   right then
```
G               |D        |G/D  D
```
   Instead of lat - er.
```
                |D                        |
```
You know, the people were quite pleased
```
             |G                          |
```
'Cause the out - law had been seized.
```
          |A               |G           |            |D            |
```
And on the whole, it was a ver - y good year   for the undertak - er.

Chorus 3

```
G/D         D              ‖A        Bm   |
```
   You know, you know, you can't talk to a man
```
      A   |    D    G   |           |
```
With a shot - gun in his hand,
```
G                  |D              G/D      ‖
```
Shotgun in his hand. (Smackwater Jack, yeah.)

Outro

D |
Smackwater Jack bought a shot - gun.

        |**D** |
Yeah, Smack - water Jack bought a shot - gun.

 |**D** | |**G/D** **D**
Oh, Smackwater Jack, yeah. (Smackwater Jack, yeah.)

     |**D** |**G/D** **D** |
Talking about Smackwater Jack, yeah.

D |
(Ooh, and his shot - gun.)

     |**D** |
Talking about Smackwater Jack, oh.

 |**D** |**G/D** **D** |
(Ooh, talking about Jack and his shot - gun.

D | |
Talking about Smack, talking about Jack,

D |**G/A** **D**   ‖
Smackwater Jack, yeah.)

So Far Away

Words and Music by
Carole King

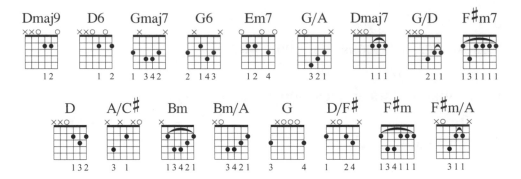

Intro   **Dmaj9   D6** |**Dmaj9   D6** |**Dmaj9   D6** |**Dmaj9   D6**

Chorus 1

‖**Dmaj9   D6** |
So far a - way.

Dmaj9   D6 |**Gmaj7   G6** |
Doesn't anybody stay in one place   anymore?

Em7   G/A |**Dmaj7 G/D Dmaj7** |
It would be so fine to see your face at my door.

Gmaj7   F♯m7   Em7   G/A |**Dmaj9   D6** |
Doesn't help   to know you're just   time a - way.

Dmaj9   D6 |**Gmaj7   G6** |
Long ago I reached for you and   there you stood.

Em7   G/A |**Dmaj7 G/D Dmaj7** |
Holding you again   could only do me   good.

Gmaj7   F♯m7   Em7   G/A |
How I wish   I could, but you're so

Dmaj9   D6 |**Dmaj9   D   A/C♯** ‖
Far a - way.

Verse 1

```
Bm                    Bm/A            |G           D/F♯ |
One more song about moving along the highway;
Em7              G/A        |Dmaj7
Can't say much of anything that's new.
 |F#m                          |Em7
If I could only work this life out     my way,
 |G/A         Bm      |Em7        G/A
I'd rather spend it     being close to you.
```

Chorus 2

```
              ‖Dmaj9      D6       |
But you're so       far a - way.

Dmaj9          D6            |Gmaj7      G6      |
Doesn't anybody stay in one place         anymore?
Em7              G/A           |Dmaj7 G/D Dmaj7     |
It would be so fine to see your face at my door.
Gmaj7    F♯m7 Em7 G/A   |Dmaj9       D6      |
Doesn't help     to know you're so      far a - way.
Dmaj9        D6         |Gmaj7       G6      |Em7 G/A       ‖
      Yeah,    you're so      far a - way.
```

Verse 2

```
G/A                    F♯m/A        |G/A                |
Traveling around sure gets me down and lonely;
Em7              G/A        |Dmaj7
Nothing else to do    but close my mind.
 |F♯m7                         |Em7
I sure hope the road don't come to     own me.
    |G/A         Bm    |Em7          |G/A
There's so many dreams    I've yet to find.
```

Chorus 3

‖Dmaj9   D6 |
But you're so   far a - way.

Dmaj9   D6 |Gmaj7   G6
Doesn't anybody stay in one place   anymore?

   |Em7   G/A |Dmaj7 G/D Dmaj7
It would be so fine to see your face at my door.

   |Gmaj7 F♯m7 Em7 G/A |Dmaj9   D6 |
And it doesn't help to know you're so   far a - way.

Dmaj9   D6 |Gmaj7   G6 |
  Yeah, you're so   far a - way.

Em7 G/A |Dmaj9   D6 |Dmaj9 D6 ‖
  Hey, you're so   far   away.

Repeat and fade

Outro   ‖:Gmaj7 G6 |Em7 G/A |Dmaj9 D6 |Dmaj9 D6 :‖

Song of Long Ago

Words and Music by
Carole King

(Capo 2nd fret)

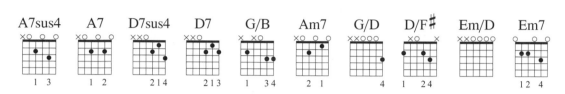

Intro   F/G |F/C   C |C/D | ||

Verse 1

G |D |
Whispering wind came un - invited,

Em |Bm7 |
Looking for somewhere else   to go.

C   Cm |Bm7   Em |
Here is a lamp   I've left   unlight - ed.

A7sus4   A7 |D7sus4   D7 |
Aren't you some - one I   should know?

F/G |C |
Memory's flame is soon   ignited,

F/G |C   G/B |
Lighting my lamp with am - ber glow.

Am7 |G/D |
Quietly friends are re - united,

C/D |G
Singing a song of long   ago.

           D/F♯ ‖**Em** |**Bm7**

Chorus 1   Na, na, na,   na,   na, na, na,

                |**F/G** |**C**

Na, na, na,   na, na, na,

         |**G**   **D/F♯** |**Em**   **Em/D**

Na, na, na, na,   na, na, na,   na, na,   na,

  |**A7**   **D7sus4** |**G**   ‖

Na, na, na, na, na, na, na.

        F/G |**G**

Bridge   Cry, cry for some - one

      |**F/G** |**G**

Who just can't be hap - py,

           |**C** |**G/B**   **Em7** |**A7sus4** **A7** |**D7sus4** ‖

And be glad you can feel   enough   to cry.

        G |**D** |

Verse 2   Younger than always, time   descended,

Em |**Bm7** |

Bringing me brand-new seeds   to sow.

C   **Cm** |**Bm7**   **Em** |

Now that they've been   a long   time plant - ed,

A7sus4   **A7** |**D7sus4**   **D7** |

What must I do   to help   them grow?

F/G |**C** |

If it had been as I intended,

F/G |**C**   **G/B** |

I wouldn't have the peace I know,

Am7 |**G/D**

Loving the people I've   befriended

  |**C/D** |**G**

And singing a song of long   ago.

Chorus 2

      D/F♯   ‖**Em** |**Bm7**

Na, na, na,   na,   na, na, na,

        |**F/G** |**C**

Na, na, na,   na, na, na,

     |**G**   **D/F♯** |**Em**   **Em/D**

Na, na, na, na,   na, na, na,   na, na,   na,

     |**A7sus4** **A7** |**D7sus4** **D7**   ‖

Na, na, na.

Verse 3

C |**G/B**   **Em7** |

As it began, so I   will end   it,

Am7   **C/D** |**G** |

Singing a song   of long ago,

C |**G/B**   **Em7**

Loving the people I've   befriend - ed

  |**Am7** |**C/D** | |**F/G** |

And singing a song of long,   long,   long a - go.

F/C **C** |**C/D** |**G**   ‖

Some Kind of Wonderful

Words and Music by
Gerry Goffin and Carole King

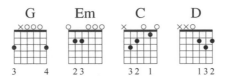

Intro

|**G** | |**Em** | |
Wonderful.   Wonderful.

|**G** | | |
Wonderful.

Verse 1

G N.C.   ‖**G** |
  All you have to do is touch my hand

|**Em** |
To show me you understand,

|**C** |
And something happens to me,

|**D** |
That's some kind of wonderful.

Verse 2

D   ‖**G** |
  At any time my little world seems blue,

|**Em** |
I just have to look at you,

|**C** |
And everything seems to be

|**D** |
Some kind of wonderful.

Bridge

||**G** | |**D** |
I know I can't express   this feeling of tenderness.

|**G** |
There's so much I wanna say,

|**C** |
But the right words don't come my way.

Verse 3

D N.C. ||**G** |
I just know when I'm in your embrace

|**Em** |
This world is a happy place,

|**C** |
And something happens to me

|**D** |
That's some kind of wonderful.

Repeat Bridge

Verse 4

D N.C. ||**G** |
I just know when I'm in your embrace

|**Em** |
This world is a happy place,

|**C** |
And something happens to me

|**D** | |**G** ||
That's some kind of wonderful.

Sweet Seasons

Words and Music by
Carole King and Toni Stern

(Capo 1st fret)

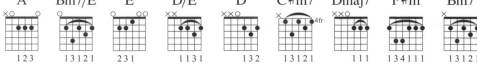

Intro

A ｜ ｜ ｜ ‖

Verse 1

A ｜

Sometimes you win, sometimes you lose,

｜A ｜ ｜

And sometimes the blues get a hold of you, ah,

Bm7/E ｜ ｜A ｜ ‖

Just when you thought you had made it.

Verse 2

A ｜ ｜

All around the block, people will talk;

A ｜

I want to give it all that I've got.

｜**Bm7/E** ｜ ｜A ｜

I just don't want, I don't want to waste it.

Chorus 1

‖E |D/E |A   D   A| |

Talking 'bout sweet sea - sons on my mind.

C♯m7 |Dmaj7

Sure does appeal to me.

    |E |F♯m |

You know we can get there ea - sily,

Bm7 |Bm7/E |A | | | ‖

Just like a sailboat sailing on the sea.

Interlude

A | | | |

A | | | |

Bm7 |C♯m7 |Dmaj7 |Bm7/E |

A | | | ‖

Verse 3

A |

Sometimes you win, sometimes   you lose,

    |A | |

And most times you choose between the two, ah,

Bm7/E | |A |

      Wondering, won - dering if you have made   it.

Verse 4

‖A |

But I'll have some kids and make my plans,

    |A |

And I'll watch the seasons running away,

    |Bm7/E | |A |

And I'll build   me a life in the o - pen, a life in the coun - try.

Chorus 2

```
         ‖E        |D/E                        |A      D     A|                |
```
Talking 'bout sweet sea - sons on my mind.

```
C♯m7                      |Dmaj7
```
Sure does appeal to me.

```
      |E                              |F♯m           |
```
You know we can get there ea - sily,

```
Bm7                  |Bm7/E                |A        |           ‖
```
Just like a sailboat sailing on the sea.

```
                                             |
```

Outro

```
         ‖A         |         |         |
```
Talking 'bout sweet   sea - sons,

```
             |A         |                     |            |
```
Talking 'bout sweet,   sweet, sweet sea - sons.

```
             |A         |         |         |
```
Talking 'bout sweet   sea - sons,

```
             |A         |         |         |           ‖
```
Talking 'bout sweet   sea - sons.

Take Good Care of My Baby

Words and Music by
Gerry Goffin and Carole King

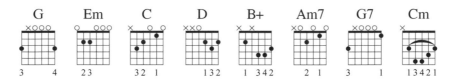

Intro

G |Em |C |D

My tears are falling 'cause you've taken her a - way.

|G |B+

And though it really hurts me so,

|C   Am7 |D ||

There's something that I've got to say:

Verse 1

G |Em |C |D |

Take good care of my   ba - by.

G |Em |C |D |

Please don't ever make her blue.

G |G7 |

Just tell her that you love her,

C |Cm |

Make sure you're thinking of her

G |Em |C |D

In every - thing you say and do.

Verse 2

‖G |Em |C |D |
Ah,   take good care of my   ba - by.

G |Em |C |D |
Now, don't you ever make her cry.

G |G7 |
Just let your love surround her,

C |Cm |
Paint rainbows all around her.

G |C   D |G | ‖
Don't let her see a cloudy sky.

Bridge

C |D
Once upon a time

  ‖G |Em |
That little girl was mine.

C |D
  If I'd been true,

 |G   Em |C   D
I know she'd never be with you.

Verse 3

‖G |Em |C |D |
So,   take good care of my   ba - by.

G |Em |C |D |
Be just as kind as you can be.

G |G7 |
And if you should discover

C |Cm |
That you don't really love her,

G |Em |C   D |G | |D |
Just send my baby back home to   me.

Verse 4

```
          ‖G          |Em          |C      |D        |
          Well,  take good care of my    ba - by.

          G          |Em               |C      |D         |
          Be just as kind as you can be.

          G              |G7                  |
          And if you should discover

          C                |Cm            |
          That you don't really love her,

          G              |Em        |C   |D   |G        |Em      |C      |D        ‖
          Just send my baby back home to    me.                                              Oh,
```

Repeat and fade

```
          ‖:G          |Em          |C      |D      :‖
```

Outro

```
          Take good care of my    ba - by.
```

Tapestry

Words and Music by
Carole King

(Capo 1st fret)

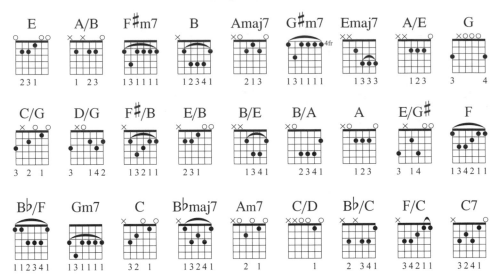

Intro

E |A/B |E |A/B |

E |A/B |E |A/B

Verse 1

‖E |A/B |E |A/B
My life has been a tapestry of rich and royal hue,

|E |A/B |E A/B |E
An everlasting vision of the ever - changing view,

|F♯m7 |B |F♯m7 |B
A wondrous woven magic in bits of blue and gold,

|Amaj7 |G♯m7 |F♯m7 |B   ‖
A tapestry to feel and see, im - possible to hold.

Verse 2

```
Emaj7                   |A/B      |Emaj7                  |A/B
```
Once, amid the soft,   silver sadness in the sky,
```
        |Emaj7          |A/B       |Emaj7 A/E    |E
```
There came a man of for - tune, a drifter passing by.
```
  |F♯m7               |B             |F♯m7                    |B
```
He wore a torn and tattered cloth a - round his leathered hide,
```
      |Amaj7      |G♯m7      |F♯m7                |B      |F♯m7  |B
```
And a coat of many colors, yellow - green on either side.

Verse 3

```
        ||G                  |C/G       |D/G       |C/G           |
```
He moved with some un - certainty, as if he didn't know
```
G                         |C/G      |D/G      C/G       |G      |
```
Just what he was there   for, or where he ought to go.
```
B                      |F♯/B          |E/B                  |B
```
Once he reached for something golden hanging from a tree,
```
      |B/E               |B/A  Amaj7  |          |   A   E/G♯  F♯m7  ||
```
And his hand come down emp - ty.

Verse 4

```
E              |A/B      |E                      |A/B
```
Soon, within my tapestry, a - long the rutted road,
```
   |E            |A/B          |E          A/B      |E
```
He sat down on a river rock and turned in - to a toad.
```
  |F♯m7               |B          |F♯m7                  |B
```
It seemed that he had fallen into someone's wicked spell,
```
      |Amaj7      |G♯m7       |F♯m7             |B             ||
```
And I wept to see him suffer, though I didn't know him well.

Verse 5

```
F                 | Bb/F          | F                      | Bb/F
As I watched in sorrow, there suddenly appeared
  | F             | Bb/F          | F         Bb/F  | F
A figure, grey and ghostly, be - neath the flowing beard.
   | Gm7                    | C          | Gm7                | C
In times of deepest dark - ness, I've seen him dressed in black.
      | Bbmaj7        | Am7         | Gm7                | C
Now my tapestry's un - raveling; he's come to take me back.
   | Gm7              | C/D         |          | Bb/C        |              ||
He's come to take me back.
```

Outro

```
F              | Bb/F          | F                 | Bb/F               |

F/C            | Bb/C      C7 | F                    ||
```

Up on the Roof

Words and Music by
Gerry Goffin and Carole King

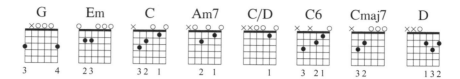

Intro   G |

Verse 1

‖G |Em
When this old world starts getting me down
  |C |Am7   C/D |G |
And people are just too much for me to face,
 |G |Em
I climb way up to the top of the stairs
  |C |Am7   C/D |G | ‖
And all my cares just drift right into space.

Chorus 1

C |C6 |Cmaj7 |C
On the roof it's peaceful as can be,
 |G |Em |C |
And there the world be - low can't bother me.
D N.C.
Let me tell you now...

Verse 2

```
    ‖G                      |Em
When I come home feeling tired and beat,
 |C              |Am7  C/D      |G                    |
I go up where the air is fresh and sweet. (Up on the roof.)
 |G                |Em
I get away from the hustling crowds
   |C              |Am7  C/D      |G              |        ‖
And all that rat race noise down in the street. (Up on the roof.)
```

Chorus 2

```
C                |C6          |Cmaj7      |C
On the roof's the only place I      know
   |G              |Em              |C
Where you just have to wish to make it so.
   |D   N.C.      |G                  |        ‖
Let's go! Up on the roof. (Up on the roof.)
```

Interlude

```
G            |Em          |C          |Am7  C/D  |G            |
```

Chorus 3

```
  ‖C                  |C6          |Cmaj7    |C
At night the stars put on a show for free,
 |G              |Em              |C        |
And, darling, you can share it all with me.
D  N.C.                    ‖
  I keep a-telling you...
```

Verse 3

```
G                          |Em
Right smack dab in the middle of town
 |C              |Am7      C/D |G                      |
I found a para-dise that's trouble-proof. (Up on the roof.)
  |G                |Em
And if this world starts getting you down,
     |C                   |Am7     C/D |G              |
There's room enough for two up on the roof. (Up on the roof.)
```

Outro

```
        ||Em                    |
Up on the roof. (Up on the roof.)
            |G                  |
Oh, come on ba - by. (Up on the roof.)
             |Em                  |
Oh, come on hon - ey. (Up on the roof.)
Em          |G                |         ||
Everything's al - right. (Up on the roof.)
```

Wasn't Born to Follow

Words and Music by
Gerry Goffin and Carole King

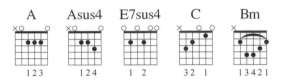

(Capo 3rd fret)

Intro

A   Asus4 A Asus4 A | Asus4 A Asus4 A |

A   Asus4 A Asus4 A | Asus4 A Asus4 A | Asus4 A

Verse 1

Asus4 A ‖ |
No,   I'd rather go and journey where the diamond crescent's flowing

     |**A** |
And run across the valleys be - neath the sacred mountain

      |**A** |
And wander through the forest where the trees have leaves of prisms

      |**E7sus4** |
That break the light up into colors

                         |**A**   Asus4 A Asus4 A |
That no one knows the names   of.

A   Asus4 A Asus4 A |A   Asus4 A

Verse 2

                     Asus4   A ‖ |
And when it's   time I'll go and wait beside the legendary fountain
          |**A** |
Till I see your form reflected in its clear and jeweled waters.
       |**A** |
And if you think I'm ready you may lead me to the chasm
                 |**E7sus4** |
Where the rivers of our visions
                               |**A**   **Asus4 A Asus4 A** | **Asus4 A**
Flow into one an - other.

Verse 3

                     Asus4   A ‖ |
And I'll   stay awhile and wonder at the mist that they've created
          |**A** |
And lose myself within it, cleanse my mind and body.
       |**A** | |
And I   know at that moment as I stand in that cathedral,
E7sus4 |
I will want to dive beneath
                               |**A**   **Asus4 A Asus4 A** | **Asus4 A Asus4 A** ‖
The white cascading wa - ter.

Interlude   **A**   **C   Bm**   **A** | | |

                 A   **C   Bm**   **A** | | |

                 E7sus4 | |**A**   **Asus4 A Asus4 A** |

                 A   **Asus4 A Asus4 A** |**A**   **Asus4 A**

Verse 4

Asus4 A ‖ | |
She   may beg and she may plead and she may argue with her logic,

A |
Mention all the things I'll lose that really have no value.

         |**A** | |
Though I doubt that she will ever come to understand my meaning,

E7sus4 |
In the end she'll surely know

                     |**A**   **Asus4 A Asus4 A** | **Asus4 A**
I was not born to   fol   -   low,

    Asus4 A | **Asus4 A Asus4 A** | **Asus4 A Asus4 A** ‖
Not born   to fol   -   low.

Repeat and fade

Intro   ‖:**A**   **Asus4 A Asus4 A** | **Asus4 A Asus4 A** :‖

Where You Lead

Words and Music by
Carole King and Toni Stern

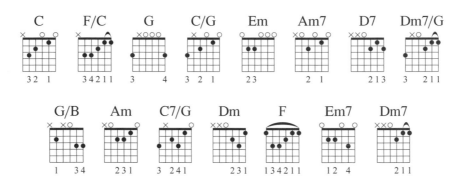

Intro

C   F/C   C | F/C   C | F/C   C | F/C   C ‖

Verse 1

   G   **|C/G**
Wanting you the way I do,
  |G   **|C/G**
I only want to be with you.
         |G   **|Em**
And I would go to the ends   of the earth
        |Am7   **D7**   **|Dm7/G**
'Cause, dar - ling, to me that's what   you're worth.

Chorus 1

           ‖**C**   **F/C**   **|C**   **F/C**
Where you lead,   I will fol - low,
         |F   **|C**
Anywhere   that you tell me to.
         |C   **G/B**   **|Am**   **C7/G**
If you need,   you need me to be   with you,
      |F Em Dm Dm7/G   **|C**   ‖
I will fol - low   where you lead.

Verse 2

```
G                         |C/G
If you're out on the road,
         |G            |C/G        |
Feeling lone - ly and so cold,
G                  |Em
All you have to do is call    my name
      |Am7    D7          |Dm7/G
And I'll be    there  on the next       train.
```

Repeat Chorus 1

Bridge

```
F                    C   |
  I always wanted a real  home
   |F                 C    |
With flowers on the window-sill,
   |F                C   |           |
But if you want to live in New  York City,
F               C   |                    |
Honey, you know I will.  (Yes, I will, yes, I will.)
F                       C  |           |
  I never thought I could get  satisfaction
F              C   |
  From just one man,
    |F          C   |               |
But if anyone could keep  me happy,
F          Em7        |Dm7   Dm7/G
  You're the one who can.
```

Chorus 2

```
              ‖C    F/C         |C      F/C
Where  you  lead,          I  will  fol - low,
         |F                  |C
Anywhere      that  you  tell   me  to.
                 |C     G/B       |Am           C7/G
If  you  need,    you  need  me  to  be      with  you,
         |F  Em   Dm   Dm7/G          |
I  will  fol - low.  (Oh.)  Oh.   (Oh.)
```

Chorus 3

```
              ‖C    F/C         |C      F/C
Where  you  lead,          I  will  fol - low,
         |F                        |C
Any,  an - ywhere  that  you  tell   me  to.
                 |C     G/B       |Am           C7/G
If  you  need,    you  need  me  to  be      with  you,
         |F  Em  Dm  Dm7/G          |C      F/C    C |        F/C
I  will  fol - low       where  you  lead.
         C |     F/C    C |     F/C        C ‖
Oh,  ba - by.               Ooh.   (Ooh.)
```

Outro

```
         ‖:C          F/C    C    |          F/C    C |
         I'm  gonna  follow  where   you  lead.
                                    Repeat and fade
         C          F/C    C    |          F/C    C :‖
         (I'm  gonna  follow  where   you  lead.)
```

Will You Love Me Tomorrow
(Will You Still Love Me Tomorrow)

Words and Music by
Gerry Goffin and Carole King

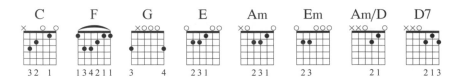

Intro

C | | | ||

Verse 1

C | |F G |
   Tonight you're mine, complete - ly;
C | |G |
   You give your love so sweetly.
   |E |
Tonight the light
|Am | |
Of love is in your eyes,
F |G |C | ||
   But will you love me to - morrow?

Verse 2

C | |F G |
   Is this a lasting treasure
C | |G |
   Or just a moment's pleasure?
   |E |
Can I believe
|Am | |
The magic of your sighs?
F |G |C | ||
   Will you love me to - morrow?

Bridge

```
F              |        |Em      |        |
   Tonight with words un - spoken,
F              |           |C      |        |
   You say that I'm the only one.
F              |     |Em     |
   But will my heart be broken.
        |N.C. Am/D        |N.C. D7  |F      |G      ||
When the night      meets the morn - ing sun?
```

Verse 3

```
C                        |F      |G      |
   I'd like to know that your love
C              |     |G        |
   Is a love I can be sure of.
   |E              |
So tell me now
   |Am              |        |
And I won't ask again.
F        |G        |C      |        ||
   Will you still love me to - morrow?
```

Interlude

```
C              |           |F      |G          |

C              |           |G          |
```

Outro

```
      ‖E            |
So  tell  me  now
       |Am              |           |
And  I  won't  ask  again.
F            |G        |C        |          |
   Will  you  still  love  me  to - morrow?
F            |G        |C        |          |
   Will  you  still  love  me  to - morrow?
F            |G        |C        |          ‖
   Will  you  still  love  me  to - morrow?
```

(You Make Me Feel Like)
A Natural Woman

Words and Music by
Gerry Goffin, Carole King and Jerry Wexler

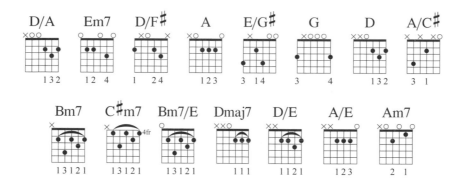

Verse 1

D/A Em7 D/F# | A | | E/G# | |
                Looking out on the morning rain,

G | | D | A/C# Bm7 |
I used to feel so unin - spired.

A | | E/G# | |
And when I knew I had to face another day,

G | | D | A/C# Bm7 |
Lord, it made me feel so   tired.

Bm7 | C#m7 |
Before the day I met you,

Bm7 | C#m7 |
Life was so un - kind.

|Bm7 | C#m7 | Bm7 |
But you're the key to my peace of mind.

Chorus 1

|Bm7/E || A |
'Cause you make me feel,

Dmaj7 | A |
You make me feel,

Dmaj7 | A N.C. | Bm7 | D/E   A/E   D/E ||
You make me feel like a natural woman (woman).

Verse 2

```
A              |               |E/G♯            |               |
   When my soul was in the lost and found,
G          |       |D      |  A/C♯          |
   You came a - long to claim it.
A              |                |E/G♯            |               |
   I didn't know just what was wrong with me,
G              |            |D      |  A/C♯  Bm7  |
   Till your kiss  helped me name it.
Bm7                  |C♯m7     |
   Now I'm no longer doubtful
Bm7                  |C♯m7     |
   Of what I'm living for,
   |Bm7              |C♯m7           |Bm7
And if I make you happy I don't need to do more.
```

Repeat Chorus 1

Bridge

```
A      |                   |Em7                      |               |
   Oh,  baby, what you've done to me (what you've done to me).
A                  |       |Em7        |               |
   You make me feel so good inside (good inside).
Dmaj7  |          |Am7         |               |
   And I just want to be (want to be)
Dmaj7                  |A/C♯           |Bm7          |
   Close to you. You make me fell so a - live.
```

Chorus 2

Bm7/E ‖**A** |
You make me feel,

Dmaj7 |**A** |
You make me feel,

Bm7/E |**A** **N.C.** | |**Bm7** |
You make me feel like a natural woman.

Bm7/E |**A** |
You make me feel,

Dmaj7 |**A** |
   You make me feel,

Dmaj7 |**A** **N.C.** | |**Bm7** |**Bm7/E** |**A** ‖
You make me feel like a natural woman (woman).

You've Got a Friend

Words and Music by Carole King

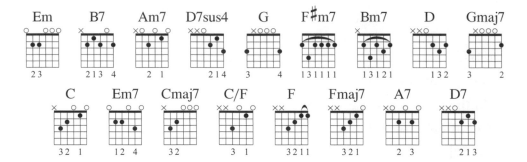

Verse 1

           |Em |B7
When you're down   and trou - bled

     |Em   B7 |Em
And you need a helping hand

    |Am7 |D7sus4 |G | |
And nothing,   woh, nothing is going right,

F♯m7 |B7
Close your eyes and think   of me

    |Em   B7 |Em
And soon I will   be there

    |Am7 |Bm7 |D7sus4 |D
To brighten up   even your darkest night.

Chorus

|G |Gmaj7
You just call   out my name,

|C |Am7
And you know wherever I am,

D7sus4 |G |Gmaj7
I'll come run - ning, oh yeah, ba   -   by,

|D7sus4 |
To see you again.

G |Gmaj7 |
Winter, spring, summer, or fall,

C |Em7
All you got to do is call

|Cmaj7   Bm7 |D7sus4
And I'll be there,   yeah, yeah, yeah.

|G |C |G |F♯m7   B7
You've got a friend.

Verse 2

‖Em |B7
If the sky   above   you

|Em   B7 |Em
Should turn dark and full of clouds

|Am7 |D7sus4 |G |
And that old   north wind   should begin to blow,

F♯m7 |B7
Keep your head togeth - er

|Em   B7 |Em |
And call my name   out loud,

Am7 |Bm7 |D7sus4 |D
Soon I will be knock - ing upon your door.

**Repeat Chorus
(omit last line)**

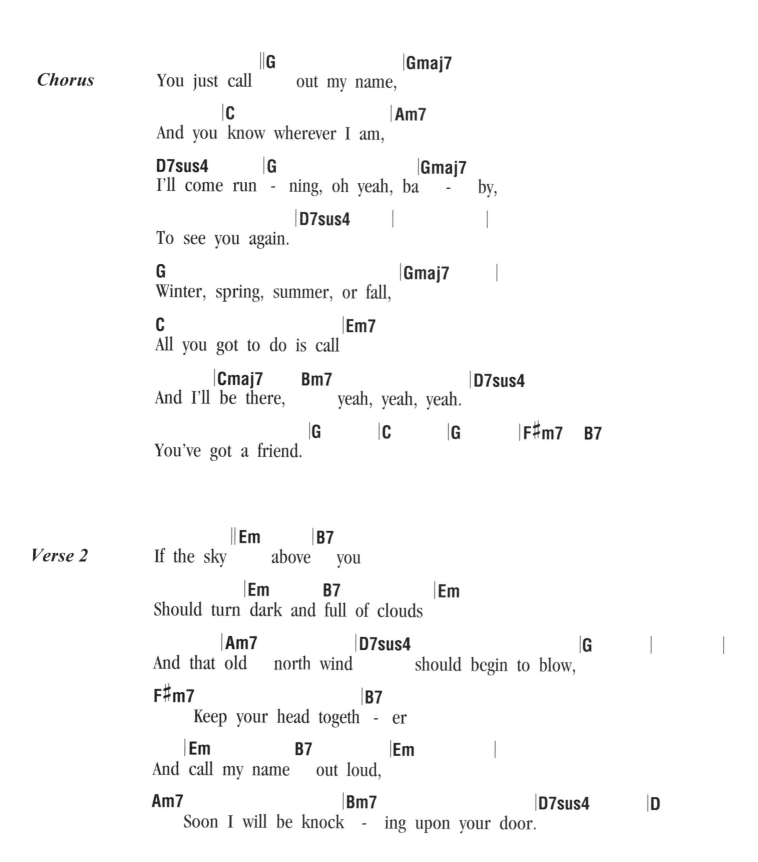

Bridge

```
      ‖C/F            F          |C
Hey, ain't    it good to know that you've got a friend

       |G                          |Gmaj7
When people can be so cold?

       |C                    |Fmaj7
They'll hurt you and desert       you.

          |Em7                      |A7
Well, they'll take your soul if you let    them.

            |D7sus4                   |D7
Oh yeah, but don't you let them.
```

**Repeat Chorus
(omit last line)**

Outro

```
                        ‖G          |C
You've got a friend.

                     |G             |
You've got a friend.

C                              |G
   Ain't it good to know you've got    a friend?

        |C                            |G
Ain't it good    to know you've got a friend?

      |C                      |G              ‖
Oh, yeah,    yeah, you've got a friend.
```

Guitar Chord Songbooks

Each 6" x 9" book includes complete lyrics, chord symbols, and guitar chord diagrams.

Acoustic Hits
00701787 . . . . $14.99

Acoustic Rock
00699540 . . . . $17.95

Alabama
00699914 . . . . $14.95

The Beach Boys
00699566 . . . . $14.95

The Beatles (A-I)
00699558 . . . . $17.99

The Beatles (J-Y)
00699562 . . . . $17.99

Blues
00699733 . . . . $12.95

Broadway
00699920 . . . . $14.99

Johnny Cash
00699648 . . . . $17.99

Steven Curtis Chapman
00700702 . . . . $17.99

Children's Songs
00699539 . . . . $16.99

Christmas Carols
00699536 . . . . $12.99

Christmas Songs
00699537 . . . . $12.95

Eric Clapton
00699567 . . . . $15.99

Classic Rock
00699598 . . . . $15.99

Country
00699534 . . . . $14.95

Country Favorites
00700609 . . . . $14.99

Country Standards
00700608 . . . . $12.95

Cowboy Songs
00699636 . . . . $12.95

Creedence Clearwater Revival
00701786 . . . . $12.99

Crosby, Stills & Nash
00701609 . . . . $12.99

John Denver
02501697 . . . . $14.99

Neil Diamond
00700606 . . . . $14.99

Disney
00701071 . . . . $14.99

The Doors
00699888 . . . . $15.99

The Best of Bob Dylan
14037617 . . . . $17.99

Early Rock
00699916 . . . . $14.99

Folksongs
00699541 . . . . $12.95

Folk Pop Rock
00699651 . . . . $14.95

Four Chord Songs
00701611 . . . . $12.99

Glee
00702501 . . . . $14.99

Gospel Hymns
00700463 . . . . $14.99

Grand Ole Opry®
00699885 . . . . $16.95

Green Day
00103074 . . . . $12.99

Guitar Chord Songbook White Pages
00702609 . . . . $29.99

Hillsong United
00700222 . . . . $12.95

Irish Songs
00701044 . . . . $14.99

Billy Joel
00699632 . . . . $15.99

Elton John
00699732 . . . . $15.99

Latin Songs
00700973 . . . . $14.99

Love Songs
00701043 . . . . $14.99

Bob Marley
00701704 . . . . $12.99

Paul McCartney
00385035 . . . . $16.95

Steve Miller
00701146 . . . . $12.99

Modern Worship
00701801 . . . . $16.99

Motown
00699734 . . . . $16.95

The 1950s
00699922 . . . . $14.99

The 1980s
00700551 . . . . $16.99

Nirvana
00699762 . . . . $16.99

Roy Orbison
00699752 . . . . $12.95

Tom Petty
00699883 . . . . $15.99

Pop/Rock
00699538 . . . . $14.95

Praise & Worship
00699634 . . . . $14.99

Elvis Presley
00699633 . . . . $14.95

Queen
00702395 . . . . $12.99

Red Hot Chili Peppers
00699710 . . . . $16.95

Rock Ballads
00701034 . . . . $14.99

Rock 'n' Roll
00699535 . . . . $14.95

Bob Seger
00701147 . . . . $12.99

Sting
00699921 . . . . $14.99

Taylor Swift
00701799 . . . . $15.99

Three Chord Songs
00699720 . . . . $12.95

Top 100 Hymns Guitar Songbook
75718017 . . . . $12.99

Wedding Songs
00701005 . . . . $14.99

Hank Williams
00700607 . . . . $14.99

Neil Young
00700464 . . . . $14.99

HAL•LEONARD®
CORPORATION
7777 W. BLUEMOUND RD. P.O. BOX 13819 MILWAUKEE, WI 53213

Visit Hal Leonard online at **www.halleonard.com**

Prices, contents, and availability subject to change without notice.

0712

AUTHENTIC CHORDS · ORIGINAL KEYS · COMPLETE SONGS

The *Strum It* series lets players strum the chords and sing along with their favorite hits. Each song has been selected because it can be played with regular open chords, barre chords, or other moveable chord types. Guitarists can simply play the rhythm, or play and sing along through the entire song. All songs are shown in their original keys complete with chords, strum patterns, melody and lyrics. Wherever possible, the chord voicings from the recorded versions are notated.

THE BEACH BOYS' GREATEST HITS
_____ 00699357............................... $12.95

THE BEATLES FAVORITES
_____ 00699249............................... $14.95

BEST OF CONTEMPORARY CHRISTIAN
_____ 00699531............................... $12.95

BEST OF STEVEN CURTIS CHAPMAN
_____ 00699530............................... $12.95

VERY BEST OF JOHNNY CASH
_____ 00699514............................... $14.99

CELTIC GUITAR SONGBOOK
_____ 00699265............................... $9.95

CHRISTMAS SONGS FOR GUITAR
_____ 00699247............................... $10.95

CHRISTMAS SONGS WITH 3 CHORDS
_____ 00699487............................... $8.95

VERY BEST OF ERIC CLAPTON
_____ 00699560............................... $12.95

COUNTRY STRUMMIN'
_____ 00699119............................... $8.95

JIM CROCE – CLASSIC HITS
_____ 00699269............................... $10.95

VERY BEST OF JOHN DENVER
_____ 00699488............................... $12.95

NEIL DIAMOND
_____ 00699593............................... $12.95

DISNEY FAVORITES
_____ 00699171............................... $10.95

BEST OF THE DOORS
_____ 00699177............................... $12.99

MELISSA ETHERIDGE GREATEST HITS
_____ 00699518............................... $12.99

FAVORITE SONGS WITH 3 CHORDS
_____ 00699112............................... $8.95

FAVORITE SONGS WITH 4 CHORDS
_____ 00699270............................... $8.95

FIRESIDE SING-ALONG
_____ 00699273............................... $8.95

FOLK FAVORITES
_____ 00699517............................... $8.95

IRVING BERLIN'S GOD BLESS AMERICA®
_____ 00699508............................... $9.95

GREAT '50s ROCK
_____ 00699187............................... $9.95

GREAT '60s ROCK
_____ 00699188............................... $9.95

GREAT '70s ROCK
_____ 00699262............................... $9.95

THE GUITAR STRUMMERS' ROCK SONGBOOK
_____ 00701678............................... $14.99

BEST OF WOODY GUTHRIE
_____ 00699496............................... $12.95

JOHN HIATT COLLECTION
_____ 00699398............................... $12.95

THE VERY BEST OF BOB MARLEY
_____ 00699524............................... $12.95

A MERRY CHRISTMAS SONGBOOK
_____ 00699211............................... $9.95

MORE FAVORITE SONGS WITH 3 CHORDS
_____ 00699532............................... $8.95

THE VERY BEST OF TOM PETTY
_____ 00699336............................... $12.95

POP-ROCK GUITAR FAVORITES
_____ 00699088............................... $8.95

ELVIS! GREATEST HITS
_____ 00699276............................... $10.95

BEST OF GEORGE STRAIT
_____ 00699235............................... $14.99

TAYLOR SWIFT FOR ACOUSTIC GUITAR
_____ 00109717............................... $16.99

BEST OF HANK WILLIAMS JR.
_____ 00699224............................... $12.95

HAL•LEONARD®
7777 W. BLUEMOUND RD. P.O. BOX 13819 MILWAUKEE, WI 53213

Visit Hal Leonard online at **www.halleonard.com**

Prices, contents & availability subject to change without notice.

0113